PLAIN TALK FOR WOMEN: THE KEY TO GETTING MARRIED AND TIPS FOR STAYING MARRIED

Elner J. Makia

First printing

Plain Talk for Women: The Key to Getting Married and Tips for Staying Married is an educational reference tool.

Published by The Educational Enhancement Group, Magnolia, Arkansas

ISBN: 0-9748753-9-2

Printed in the United States of America

For additional copies, contact:
        The Educational Enhancement Group
        P.O. Box 935
        Magnolia, Arkansas 71753
        (870) 234-0535
        E-mail: edu_group04@yahoo.com

Cover Artwork by Communications Center, Southern Arkansas University

Layout by David Wingfield, Department of English and Foreign Languages, Southern Arkansas University

Dedication/Acknowledgements

I dedicate this book to all females who eagerly want to get married and to all married couples. My greatest thanks go to the members of the Jackson Street Church of Christ, Magnolia, Arkansas, and to other participants who willingly responded to both questionnaires for this book. And to my husband, Japhet Ndumbe, I thank you sincerely for the many hours you spent editing *Plain Talk for Women*.

Contents

PLAIN TALK FOR WOMEN: THE KEY TO GETTING MARRIED AND TIPS FOR STAYING MARRIED

Elner J. Makia

The Educational Enhancement Group

ABOUT THE AUTHOR

Elner J. Makia's academic accomplishments include postmaster's certifications in counseling and in career orientation, a Master of Science in human development and family studies, and a Bachelor of Science in family and consumer sciences. She served 10 years as a vocational high school teacher and junior high career orientation teacher in the Arkansas Public School system. Makia was also an adjunct graduate faculty at Southern Arkansas University (SAU), where she taught counseling classes and was Counselor/Tutor Coordinator for the Alternative Multicultural Nighttime Tutoring Center at SAU. She is currently a high school counselor. Makia resides in Magnolia, Arkansas, with her husband and two children. She believes that life is a journey, and each person is in search of peace and fulfillment, which can be accomplished through one's complete knowledge of God and His mercies.

Preface

The first part of this book is designed to help all unmarried females who have a desire to be married, and the second part provides valuable tips to those married so they can stay in harmony with their spouses—together in a conjugal relationship—as our Great God intended. I realize that in today's society, not all women want to be married. However, there are many, despite their career successes, who have a void in their existence because of their unmarried status. It is to this group I have written the first part of this book. My aim is not to put unmarried women down but to help those desiring betrothment learn some techniques that will better their chances of getting married. If you keep reading the book, I believe you will pick up some important information—the key that will greatly increase your chances of getting married (most probably to the right person).

The second part of *Plain Talk for Women* provides important tips to the couple that has taken the pertinent vow of matrimony. Once the man and woman so commit themselves, they are supposed to become indivisible; that is, the husband and the wife form a unit, a couple. This does not, however, mean that this man and this woman are bound to each other with blistering fetters but with the bonds of love—bonds that no mortal force can destroy. So marriage is a commitment between two persons, preferably male and female. This commitment is a bond that strengthens over time. Please utilize the information in this book to the best of your ability, and I wish you a blessed marriage partner and longevity in your relationship.

Elner J. Makia

PART 1

PLAIN TALK FOR WOMEN: THE KEY TO GETTING MARRIED

CHAPTERS ONE THROUGH FOUR

CHAPTER ONE
KNOW YOURSELF

A. Values

B. Goals

C. Biological Make-up

Chapter 1: Know Yourself

One of the most important reasons some women do not get married is because they do not know themselves. When women are asked to describe themselves, some may respond by saying, "I am black" or "I am white." This means that they are identifying themselves with skin tone. That doesn't say a lot. Next, some may go into lengthy details about their height, hair color, and physical stamina. Well, these are all good and fine attributes; but, basically, that is a lot of empty information. There are so many women similar in skin tone, hair coloring, and height that if a guy has seen one, he has basically seen them all.

Therefore, if you start out by assessing yourself on a physical sphere, then you are technically seeing yourself on the surface as a man may see you—a piece of meat ready for him to eat. Once you are eaten and digested, he forgets you, waiting for the next round or serving. Now, were you to take the same statement from a different perspective, you should really assess yourself and realize that you embody more than flesh and bones and charisma. You could be the lady with the desire to help impart world peace, prevent starvation in your neighborhood, or cure patients suffering from serious illnesses.

Maybe now you are beginning to see that a female incorporates her mysticism of uniqueness, not only by the perfume she wears or the tone of her voice but also (and especially) by her inner perception of who she really is. Once she knows what's important to her, then she will be able to act upon her basic instincts, and a lot of the shallowness that intrudes will be obliterated and not used against her in the meat market. With the knowledge of her own supremeness, flowery words that a man may issue without substance will not be able to sway her into a premature offering of her virginity as a dessert on the main course of some male's Thanksgiving meal.

A. Values

Ladies, knowing yourself means understanding what is important to you; this stems from your values. The older females may help teach the younger ones values even if the girls' parents did not, especially if their mothers neglected to do so. Mothers, teach your daughters to value themselves, and they won't always measure their self-worth by a male's consumption of them. Teach them to love both their inner as well as their outer portions because the internal workings of their minds and thoughts are more significant than the formation of their breasts or hips or legs. Also, teach your girls from birth on up how to reach beyond the level of being held by their fathers and told they are okay. I am really stressing the mother's role because if she neglects her job, then the tendency is for her daughters not to know any better than to give up their virginity whenever and wherever—on demand. Ladies, you must realize that we are God's gift to the universe, so we must set high standards for ourselves and believe that God intends to use our presence in this world for a purpose.

A gift is not something that is stolen through flattery and lies. So learn how to decipher truth from deception. When you value yourself as a diamond in the rough, then you realize that you are beautiful externally and internally. Also, males may see the roughness but yearn for the inner brilliance of the diamond. Don't allow them to have that shine until marriage. Nevertheless, if women do not believe in their price, then they allow men to remove the dirt from the diamond before paying the full price. When this happens, females contribute to the cycle of disrespect that some men may have for them.

B. Goals

Take some time, sit down, and discover your objectives instead of becoming clones of the male species. If you desire a husband, kids, and a life of fulfillment, set goals—things you can try to accomplish. Goal setting helps one develop inner depth and individualism. A specific goal should be one that exists outside the realm of attracting male attention. Goals should be centered on showcasing your unique feminism in the form of concrete undertakings as finishing grade school, high school, and college; passing the standardized exams and getting scholarships which would lead you to becoming self-actualized and reaching your highest level of attainment or perfection.

Exist outside of the male clicking system, and you will find that you are getting closer to one of your ultimate goals, marriage. How? Because where there is pollen, there is a bee. In comparison, a woman who is self assured, not just playacting but one confident with her whole personality, draws eligible male species for marriage as the pollen draws the bee. For instance, try having a conversation with a decent male. He will start out on an intellectual level. If he glimpses any trace of uncertainty in the female, he stores this information for future use against the female, which will inadvertently aid him in getting into her storehouse of goods. So what has he done? He has played on her slackness and sampled the honey before buying the entire jar. After all, who wants to keep a pretty eggshell when one has eaten the valuable goodness inside?

Females, be very sure that your inside package is just as brilliant and compact as the outside. What does this mean? It means THINK, BELIEVE, and ACT according to the knowledge that God has given you. Don't allow some serpent to dribble and manipulate you into rendering your most prized possession to him before you are actually ready to do so. That's why you are labeled MOTHER EARTH. You can rule and have all your desires if you believe in yourself, not just the outward portion of you. That's like money you can take to the bank and cash!

C. Biological Make-Up

LADIES, KNOW YOUR OWN BODIES. What's sad is that women walk around not even understanding how their bodies work. And this lack of knowledge of their own biological make-up may be one of the factors prohibiting potential suitors from knocking at many ladies' doors.

How do you understand your body? Well, it would be helpful for mothers to sit down with their daughters and explain to them the intricate workings of their reproduction system. This would be ideal. Unfortunately, most mothers are ignorant and embarrassed about the workings of their own bodies. They are not confident in their own sensuality and uninformed about factors related to their own pregnancies. All they know is that they had an intimate relationship with their boyfriend or husband; and, a couple of weeks later, they were pregnant. Come on, we need to know more than this. Get a book, explore, and take a biology or an anatomy/physiology class if you have to. In the final analysis, if mothers don't learn and teach their daughters about their anatomy, the daughters will discover how it works from a man's perspective (not a male teacher or professor, however), and that is definitely not the way they should learn how the female anatomy works.

Never fear; here is the simplest explanation of how your body works. Sit down with your daughters and explain it to them. Between the ages of eleven and thirteen, for some girls, there will be some noticeable changes taking place in the female's physical anatomy. For instance, the chest will start enlarging and protruding outward. When this happens, the young lady should know that she would automatically get more attention than she may desire or even want. This is a physical change anyone can see. However, there are changes happening inside the female's body that the naked eyes cannot be seeing. A female has a reproductive system which includes uterus, fallopian tubes, ovaries, and vagina. When hormones start roaming around in the female's body, they cause things to happen. The vagina is the canal leading from the uterus to the opening outside the body. Then there are two ovaries where eggs are produced. Every female also has fallopian tubes, which conduct the egg from the ovary to the uterus, and the uterus, of course, is the organ used to nourish the young embryo during the embryo's development. The female may not even be aware of all these activities taking place in her body. Each month an egg is released due to the hormonal changes inside the body. If the female does not engage in any intimate relationship with the male during the time this egg is being released, then the egg successfully exits the body. This exiting of the egg is called menstruation.

Nevertheless, if a female, especially a teenage girl with a vibrant life ahead of her, chooses to engage in pre-marital relationships (and un-protected) during this releasing of the egg, she runs the risk of changing her life's status permanently. How does this happen? Well, the egg meets with a foreign substance (contributed by the male) that she allowed to invade her body. (Sadly, this can also happen when some deranged man rapes a female.) This festered egg, instead of leaving the woman's body, travels with the help of the motion from the fallopian tubes all the way to the uterus and attaches itself to the lining of the uterus and begins to de-velop. This is not a bad process, however. In fact, it is a miracle designed by God to be utilized within the bounds of matrimony.

But, because we live in an imperfect world, not everyone will be married as a virgin. Thus, women, in order to have a better chance of getting married, do not allow foreign particles of any kind, whether you are protected or not, to invade your temple until a man has committed himself to you in matrimony. If unmarried women allow this invasion of their costly possession, then, technically, they are helping to degrade the female species by allowing freedom of taste and liberality. In order to increase your chances of getting married, know how your body works and keep your liberality non-liberal. Remember, freely given, freely re-ceived, and easily tossed.

CHAPTER TWO

CHAPTER TWO
EXPRESS YOURSELF

A. Talk
B. Walk
C. Dress
  1. Hair
  2. Clothes
  3. Make-up
  4. Personal Hygiene
D. Act
  1. Dating
  2. Church
  3. School
  4. Work
  5. Social Gatherings

Chapter 2: Express Yourself

Besides knowing yourself, another important facet of your personal make-up is to be able to express yourself. This simply means that you are able to say what you need to say at the appropriate time. Expression of oneself can be verbal or nonverbal and is manifested in the way one talks, walks, dresses, and acts.

A. Talk

In today's society, the way a female talks says a lot about who she is. To make it in business or a chosen profession and to climb to the top of the career ladder, learning the rules of grammar is a foregone conclusion. Proper pronunciation is in, and country diction is out in many cases. Unless you are a professional or motivational speaker, who can manipulate the language to suit the mood of the audience, be straightforward in what you say. If you mean yes, say yes, but if you mean no, say no. However, you must realize that some men may feel threatened when a female is assertive, especially through her articulation. Don't let this bother you; keep on becoming the best that you can be. If grammar is one of your shortcomings, take a college course in English, or go to the Adult Education Center and refresh yourself in this area. If you don't want to get so involved, then go to the library and check out a grammar handbook to help improve your public speaking.

Also, watch the tone of voice that you use because sometimes when you speak exceptionally loud, you may come across as arrogant and unlearned. When you speak too softly, however, you may also come across as timid and shy, and men will use that as a weakness against you and try to take advantage of you. Therefore, you must learn to pitch your tone with the proper pronunciation so that you relate as one who is totally in charge of herself and of any situation. A moderate tone is desired. And, honey, if you have a very deep voice, practice raising it a pitch or two because sounding unfeminine is totally uncool to some men. The final word on talking is that you never over talk. Don't be a chatterbox who just can't shut up her trap. That is distasteful and unladylike; and, as a final thought, get rid of the vulgar words—GDH's, B'S, MF'S. No decent male wants to marry a hood rat! If you are not one and do not want to be thought of as one, then do not talk like one. Talk respectfully, and men will respect you. Trust me.

B. Walk

What in the world happened to grace—the ability to glide across the room in fluid motion? Many women today walk as army commanders. So that may be their profession, but they do not have to turn into Rambos. Women, if you want to attract and keep male species to the point of marriage, stop walking too manly—taking hard, boot stomping, snake killing steps. If the only walking you have learned is to pimp, quit please. Many guys are attracted to opposites, not sameness. When I talk about gliding across the room, I more or less mean strutting, not twisting your hips gregariously like a hooker on 24th street. Walk with dignity and pride. This reflects your inner concept that you are somebody and, in doing so, not just any shallow minded man will approach you. If you walk with charm and sensual sophistication, then you are more apt to draw the "king" of the bees than the drones. The drones may probably be interested, but your personality will most likely keep them away.

There are many classes designed to help women learn how to walk. Some courses do not appeal to all ladies. Tall, short, thin, and heavyset women of all races and nationalities can walk as beauty queens. If you do not want to take a class in posture and walking, then follow these simple steps: Stand against a door when you are at home. Put a solid object, non-breakable, on the top of your head. Move slowly away from the door, with the object still on your head. Continue to walk forward. Repeat these steps until you learn how to walk with the object on your head without dropping it. Keep your back straight throughout the process. This exercise teaches you to align your body so that you do not slouch or bend when you walk. The total picture is one of elegance, especially when you have heels on. Ladies, the length of the skirt also flatters your new walk. Remember, don't get sleazy with the skirts and start wearing them to your panty line. Now, that is tacky.

C. Dress

Being well dressed is not a figment of one's imagination. Women should look good at least 95% of the time. When I talk about being well dressed, I am looking at the whole individual. This means that women should look good from head to toe; this embodies hair, clothes, make-up, and personal hygiene.

1. Hair

Starting with the head, a hairdo can make or break a woman's appearance. All women have something in common. It may take one group longer than the other to get their hair together; nevertheless, a woman's hair is her glory, so please take care of that glory. Some women go to the grocery store looking rather shabby partly because they don't have time to fix their hair. Big, mistake! If you have a perm (for instance) that is not combed, don't go anywhere with your hair sticking straight up on the top of your head. Some parts of the hair may be nappy and some straight. This makes you look so unkempt. And to make matters worse, some women put a grooming comb in the back of their heads. What is the reason for this? I know I am addressing woman quite heartily.

And why in the world would a female put weave in her head and leave the tracks showing? If you don't know how to weave your hair properly, go to a beautician so that she/he can put it in right. Better yet, fix your own hair regardless of how short it is. When you decide to wear braids, please moisturize them so they don't look ragged and worn out. A braid spray is good to use for moisture. Sad to say, don't walk around with big flakes of dandruff showing on your scalp and on your clothes. Wash your hair, get some medicated shampoo, and eat nutritious meals to help eliminate this problem. Whatever you do, take care of your hair.

Most men are really turned off by a woman with dirty hair. Women should learn to take better care of their hair; nevertheless, I have noticed that just because some hair is long and stringy doesn't mean that it doesn't need a perm; and, for goodness sake, wash the hair regularly. When it is not washed, the stringy hair has a peculiar odor that is very unattractive. Again, guys are turned off by unpleasant odors. Also, some women are stuck in the early 60's and 70's with their hairdos. Teasing the hair and then spraying it to death with hair spray makes it look like a spider web basket. If your beautician is uninformed about new styles of the 21st century, find someone else. With technology and new advancement, women should keep up with some of the changes in hair grooming. However, remember not to get too punked out with the hair. Some women who have naturally dark hair, instead of enjoying it, make the mistake of dying it blond. Get real and be yourself; even if you change your eye contour, that will still not be compatible with blond hair. The ethnicity is still there.

Women, most men like for you to be what you are and who you are. But if you are a natural blond, God bless you. Most men are impressed with soft hair. Very feminine hairstyles get their attention every time. I believe the head of a woman is the first thing that most men notice. Keep it neat and attractive, even if you do not have fancy salon money.

2. Clothes

A woman's body is the most sacred part of her anatomy. The way in which she covers it is very important to her personality. There are many occasions when she changes her style of dressing. For instance, there are daywear, eveningwear, special occasion wear, and work wear. It does not matter the occasion; being well dressed is the key. Often, body shape or size has a lot to do with what a woman chooses to wear. Whatever her size or shape, there are garments that will bring out the best in an individual.

The first step to becoming a well-dressed woman is to know what looks good on you. Just because it is fashionable does not mean that you can wear it. How does it look for a 250-pound female to wear spandex or skimpy tops? She would look tacky. However, a good apparel that adequately covers her body parts would make her look very chic. Good taste is a remedy for any situation related to dress. Color, shape, proportion, texture, and emphasis are other things to take into consideration when considering dress. If you are not familiar with these design techniques, there are consultants who specialize in advising women about aspects related to dress. Money does not have to be a factor in being well dressed. The public library and home economics department in your area have resources about dressing.

Loving yourself is the basis for becoming a well-dressed female. Stand in front of your mirror without any clothes on. If you accept and like what you see, then you are on your way. On the other hand, if you do not like what you see, then change the things that you can and accept the ones that you cannot. For instance, if you see overweight and you aren't satisfied, visit your doctor; get on a healthy food and exercise plan. But if you see thinness and you are not satisfied, follow the same procedure as above. If your height bothers you, you cannot change that, so just accept it and move on. When you have learned to like and love yourself, then you are ready to dress the outside because you have dealt with the inside.

Shopping can be a very expensive procedure, or it can be well within whatever budget you have. Purchase the clothes that would bring out your best features. Dress as a lady, and you will feel as a lady; that, in turn, will help you act as a lady.

Many women want to get married, yet they dress as if they are working on the corner. They surely attract a lot of male attention, but it is the wrong type of attention. The guys are coming not for marriage but for a piece of what is being advertised. I am not saying that you can't wear cute little short skirts and sometimes cute little tops. What I am saying is that your style of dress represents you and your beliefs. If you dress like a slut, even if you are not, to much of the world, you are. Don't be fooled; most men want to marry respectable looking women. Get a grip on yourself; throw away many of those undersized clothes (or give them to charity), and get some that are tasteful and that fit you well. If you do this, Congratulations! You are moving forward to becoming a better you!

3. Make-Up

Another part of being well dressed is taking care of the skin, from the face to the rest of the body. A soft, youthful looking face is always a plus. In order to keep the face looking fresh, wash it with a good cleanser that is not harsh but complements the skin type. Then moisturize the face. I know many women go through the regiment of harsh masks and astringents. These products are okay, depending on your skin type and what the dermatologists recommend.

Nevertheless, before purchasing all these expensive harsh products, consult your doctor or beauty consultant. Some women do have skin problems, but most men admire beautiful, soft looking skin. When the facial skin has been cleansed and moisturized, make-up is the next step. Make-up is meant to enhance the natural facial tone of the female, not cover it up. The idea is not to put on a mask because when the mask comes off, people may wonder who you are. Therefore, keep in mind that less is better. A very light foundation, if any at all, will suffice. But be careful that you do not get happy and shade your eyelids in such a manner that you look like a creature from a horror movie. Eyeliner is okay but not necessarily needed. Please do not take the eyeliner and outline the lips. For goodness sake, people know what lips are. Again, a color that complements your skin is good. Your lips are meant to be appreciated, not caked to the point of no recognition.

Experiment and find out what looks good on you. There are all kinds of looks. Some women may go for the dramatic but for some the simplistic. Regardless of the look, make sure it is in good taste and for the right occasion. If you have no experience with make-up, some major department stores have beauty consultants to assist you. Other avenues are cooperative extension workers and family and consumer scientists (home economics teachers) who are present in almost every school district in your area. Talk to any man, and I think he will tell you that he prefers a natural looking woman. This doesn't mean that you have to be a plain Jane, but be proud of the skin that God gave you and enhance it, not hide it with excessive make-up.

4. Personal Hygiene

When a woman picks the right clothing and the right make-up, she is still not completely dressed until she has taken care of her body. You may say, "We already know this." However, you would be surprised to realize that many women are still walking around with smelling bodies and turning men off. With all the various products on the market, there is no excuse for a slovenly stinking female.

Cleanliness is next to Godliness. Wash the body! Soap and water are the most common items needed to get it clean. It doesn't matter if you have a little money or a lot; being clean is easy. Soap is very cheap, and water is plentiful, at least in many parts of the world. On basic terms, take the soap, mix it with water, and scrub under the arms, wash the lower body portions. After this is done, put on deodorant, and if there is a tendency for a strong body odor due to perspiration, use antiperspiration. Okay, so there isn't any money for deodorant and antiperspiration. No problem! Get some baking soda and rub it under your armpits. This will help keep you fresh after your bath. Men like fresh, good smells, not pungent odors. Keep in mind that bees are drawn to the pretty, fresh smelling flowers, not the decaying ones.

Please forgive me, but I must touch on this. When it is that time of the month, and you know what time I am talking about, take extra care of yourself. Women should never walk around with a strong menstrual odor. Change those pads or tampons frequently. Whatever you spend your money on, make allowance for these special items. The worst sign of a female's lack of self-esteem is when she is walking around and the men around her know that she is having a period because she has failed to take pride in herself and controlled this peculiar type of body odor. Some things are best guessed at or never known than publicized for the world. Bad impressions once made are difficult to erase.

Be proud of being a female and take care of your cleansing needs accordingly. After you have cleansed the face and body, then you can put on those to-die-for clothes that flatter, and you are ready to step out. You will find out that being well dressed says, "I like who I am, all of me: lock, stock, and barrel." Believe me, honey, men know quality, and they prefer quality to quantity. "Checkmate!"

D. Act

"Actions speak louder than words" as the old saying goes. How should a female act? This seems to be the number one question. Well, there is not just one answer because different situations call for different actions. There are actions related to dating, church, school, work, and social gatherings. As we women develop and grow, we find that our actions, in a sense, also give people an in-depth look at who we are. For now, let's talk about the various actions.

1. Dating

The purpose of dating is to go out with someone of the opposite sex (preferably). What precipitates your meeting? First of all, be conscious of who you are at all times: in the store, in the park, and in any place that you are. Do not go to these places specifically to meet men because your life has more meaning than that. Nevertheless, when you walk into a room and men are present, do not seek out their attention. Believe me; they see you. They notice you from head to toe the minute you step into the room. Avoid eye contact at all cost. Nothing turns a guy off more than eyeballing him to death. In a split minute, a man can make up his mind if he is going to approach you or not. In the event that he does not, big deal! It is his loss.

Always think positive. Never put yourself down. You don't really need a man to accomplish important things in life; however, men are a part of life, especially in the matrimonial sphere, but you don't have to get psycho just because they have not approached you. In the event that they do approach you, stay calm. After all, he is just a man. He may be looking good, smelling good, and saying the right pick-up lines. Examine what he is really saying. Indeed, everything that sparkles isn't diamond.

Okay, he asked for your name, address, and phone number; then you decide that he might be someone whom you want to get to know better. You two arrange a date. Stop being anxious; allow him to pick you up. Even though you are a career girl (hopefully), there is nothing wrong with waiting for the man to open the door for you. At all times, be a lady. Check this out: Why should you run to open your own door? Why should you run to pay for your half of the dinner? What are you running so much for? Is that your way of making him appreciate you? Chill, the man is interested, and you don't have to show him that you are a liberated female. It doesn't matter if he pays for your dinner or opens your door. Chivalry hasn't ended; and, secretly, men enjoy doing those things. Relax, and if a man is ungracious enough not to open your door or pay for a simple dinner, then believe that if you become serious with him and by chance you decide to marry him, watch out. With this attitude, he may or may not be gracious enough to take responsibility for his actions in the marriage. Hold on, even if he buys you dinner or some pretty gadgets and opens your door, this is not your ticket to allow him to sample the goods.

Enjoy the date, evaluate the situation, and simply wait and see where the dating is leading. Hopefully, it is not leading to the bedroom first but to a greater fulfillment where love and understanding await both of you.

2. Church

Going to church in many societies is accepted as the norm. People go to church for different reasons. Many go to worship our Lord and Creator. Some go to show off their outfits, others go to watch the behavior of the congregation, and still others go to hunt out perspective partners. I advise women to go to church for the right reasons. Spirituality should be a vital part of a female's holistic realm. Ladies need stability and strength, and religion provides this for many who are willing to draw upon the power of God. Whatever you believe, know that God understands what it is that you want and desire. He will fulfill all your needs. Prayer and supplication will help you get through the bad times. Have an honest desire to know God and what His word says about marriage and its promises. When most men get ready to marry, a spiritual woman is usually on their agenda. Don't be spiritual just because you want to get a husband; however, try to understand the true meaning of the word of God.

You can choose to agree or disagree with me, but I want you to know that if you truly understand what it takes to be religious, then God will give you the husband of your dreams without your having to look very far. Some ladies may say, "Who is God? I have waited this long, but He hasn't given me a man yet." God is the creator of all our lives. He sent His Son, Jesus, to die for our sins so that we may have life abundantly. Jesus is the Prince of Peace; whatever we so desire, we send our prayers to Him, and He will intercede for us to the Heavenly Father, God. Not only that, Jesus and His power enable us to walk by faith in God.

Church is a place where one unwinds and releases pent up emotions. If perhaps you do meet some man who you feel would be adequate for sharing your life, make sure he has a deep-rooted belief in God. Go with him to church so both of you may understand the full meaning of the word Christian. When you do this, you will find that happiness involves many more things than just marriage; nevertheless, marriage is a vital part of life. Just going to church with your prospective husband is not enough. You cannot become slack in your relationship with God. However, you do not have to be a virgin to get married to a great man. God is merciful enough to forgive us of our past transgressions. Repent of your sins, and ask Him to bless you with a godly and loving husband. Consider the passage in Ephesians chapter 5: 22 which states that wives should submit themselves to their husbands. Many women in our society do not want to think of themselves as submissive. The passage is very clear; in fact, this makes for a better marriage, because regardless of the position or power a woman attains, she should still look unto her husband. This does not make her weak but stronger because she can live within the kind of relationship that God and the Church approve.

But, ladies, this does not also mean that you should remain in a relationship where the man is constantly abusing you verbally and/or physically. The reason for not staying in this type of situation is because Ephesians also states that husbands must love their wives as they (husbands) love their own bodies. A man would not hurt himself; therefore, if he is hurting you and putting your life in physical, mental, and spiritual danger, then you don't need him. See the Church as a sanctuary or place of peace.

3. School

Education is a vital part of a woman's life. It is important to be intelligent and to use the knowledge that God has given you. Slumping around and being dependent is not the way to maintain independence. Many young women in society do not even finish high school. Why? Some may wonder. There are several reasons, but I believe the major one stems again from a lack of foresight—not having clear objectives and goals. When these are lacking, a female is likely to transfer positive objectives toward negative ones. Drugs, alcohol, and sex are primary reasons why most people don't complete at least a basic education. But whatever the reason, dropping out of school is a bad move.

One of the advantages of a proper education is that it will start you out on the ladder of success by helping you become financially stable. Many young women get sidetracked because of fantasies. They meet young men and consider themselves head over heels in love with such men. Love may be a warm feeling or a strong sense of bonding between two individuals. Great! However, love for someone should not supersede advancement in life. As early as ninth grade, some girls forego their education; that is very sad, indeed. They meet a boy (may be 15-18 years of age) and he sweet-talks them into lowering their guards. They have illicit sex with these boys and believe that they have a stable relationship. In the event of pregnancy, which occurs quite frequently especially today, the relationship ends. Not all the time, but in many instances, the boy continues with his training because he has no skills that would enable him to provide for two other individuals in the form of wife and child. (Or sometimes he may get himself in trouble with the law and end up in jail. This is also happening a lot today.) On the other hand, the female has nine months of preparation for motherhood, beginning another phase of her young life. Inadvertently, she struggles with the embarrassment of being pregnant and continuing school or dropping out and becoming a full time mom. Nevertheless, there are a few males, young or not, who would step in and fulfill their responsibility of being a dad. But this is all so unnecessary at such an early age for both sexes. Things would be different if they would just be friends: date in a platonic way, enjoy being in school together, and study together without sexual involvement. Some may argue that sex is not the culprit. Well, it may not be, but in many cases, it is, and if you were to speak with these young females who have been affected by not properly understanding the consequences of pre-marital sex and the effects on their education, they would probably tell you what I am telling you after their having undergone the stress of being parents before they were ready.

People may think that all college females would act differently from high school girls. Again, many are smart, but there is an ever-growing segment of the college population of women that gets caught up with sororities and fraternities, with big sisters and big brothers system on campus that these women forget the full purpose of being in college. On many university campuses, the older males, juniors and seniors, who have almost completed their first degree, would spot the entering freshman females. They may be serious about a relationship, but many times these young, adult males are just looking for fresh, young meat to sample. Please be aware, ladies, that when you go to college, go for a specific reason—to better your bargaining power in the world of work. Don't go to college in order to meet a man because you will certainty meet many men, but are they the right kind? And remember, some of them are there to meet women also, not necessarily for marriage but for good timing. If you meet a young man on campus, look into the situation fully, decipher what his goals are and if they are in synch with yours. Be cautious and keep your eyes on the prize—your degree—and make plans not to stop there but to continue to the highest level that you can attain. You will give yourself a pat on the back for maintaining your dignity and integrity. If God has deemed a man on campus worth your time and energy, he will reveal himself to you and show you that his intention is to share your mind for a lifetime and not just your body for a season.

Once you get the degree that you have set for yourself through hard work and diligence, make use of it. Do not go through all those years of schooling to sit down on your butt. Present yourself in such a way that you get a good job able to support yourself without relying on a man. God gave you talents to make a way for yourself and to serve your community. With your degree, you may also stand the chance of getting an educated man. However, it doesn't mean that only well educated women are bound to find good men. But such women generally have a better quality of life than those with little or no education, especially in this 21st century.

4. Work

    Women have a definite position in the work world. They can go as far as their academic endeavors take them. Forget about the myth that a female has to show some legs or breasts to get ahead or that she has to undermine her chastity by knocking boots with the President or CEO of the company. Okay, there might be a handful of such ladies; but, for most, all it takes is for them to use their brains. Before a female goes to work, she should make sure she refers back to the part about dress. She wants to dress appropriately for work. If she wants to be thought of as a competitive partner, she must act as one. This means that she does not have to laugh for every occasion or be super nice if the situation does not merit niceness. She does not have to be bitchy either.

    The major problem with women in the job force is jealousy. Instead of being proud of the accomplishments of each other, some women strive to discredit others, and this may hold them back in the world of work. Then they start to compete for the attention of the males on the job site. They flirt and flounce around the guys as if they were teenagers in high school. What they may not know or even suspect is that these same guys whom they are making a fool of themselves over may be in the break room talking about them. If you make the mistake of sleeping with one of these men, the office and all the departments may know about the indiscretion.

    Work is not a place to get your hook up. It is a place where you put into action all the skills that you have picked up in school. Shine in the office as a force, not as a tension releasing mechanism after a male board meeting. Act with dignity at all times. You are somebody even if the men at work tell you that you are not mainly because you won't give them some. If you try very hard to get a promotion and you do not, meet with your supervisor and outline your positive aspects and your reasons for deserving a promotion. If you are still not appreciated, then start looking for a position where you will be. However, do not start cursing and swearing and giving yourself a bad name by acting unladylike. No job is worth sacrificing your good name and your dignity. Eventually, hard work will pay off.

    Most men are turned on by the independence in a female. Now, I am not saying that you must have a college degree and the highest paying job before a male is attracted to you. What I am saying is that even if you finished only high school and have a job paying minimum wage, you are still somebody, so you do not need a man just for the purpose of supporting you. Therefore, do not go looking for a man strictly for financial reasons, but work to take care of yourself. And act as a professional at work. Even if the job is the lowest paying in the world, you can still be esteemed, and men notice respectability; in fact, they crave it. So if you go to work with vital body parts hanging out, you are going to get noticed. And if you act desperate on the job, you are bound to receive some groping and mauling from men. I do not think this will lead to a life mate. The Bible states that having faith alone without works is dead. However, keep the faith that you will find a good man, and work hard to fulfill your own needs and desires, and these aspects will attract him faster than if you were freely offering your wares.

5. Social Gatherings

Social gatherings are places that can be fun and exciting. At these places, everyone is watching everyone else to see what they will say or do. The gathering may extend anywhere from a tea party to a disco or from a talent show to a fish fry. Regardless of the occasion, protocol is expected of females. Here, people tend to be more relaxed and easygoing. Join in the fun; but, remember, you are still on display. Men will be at these events; and, sometimes, they will be scoping out the females. If you are there, do not appear too anxious to be approached by males. Again, do not crave eye contact, but remain somewhat aloof. Food is usually served at some of these occasions. The food is there to be sampled and eaten. However, some females go too far. They have a tendency to pile food sky high on their plates. Then they sit down and proceed to eat, smacking their lips and licking their fingers. My goodness, what male would want to talk to you when you are talking and food is seen in your mouth? That looks gross and nasty. Keep your mouth closed as you chew your food. If someone asks you a question while you are eating, wait until you have swallowed most of the food before you answer. Anyway, you are not supposed to have so much food in your mouth at one time.

Social gatherings also have drinks, which can range from non-alcoholic to very strong liquors. Be particular about what you drink. There is nothing more disgusting than a drunken female. Also, I am sure your mother warned you about drinking and leaving your drink and then coming back to get it. Anything can happen to it between the time you leave and the time you return. For instance, if you are at a nightclub, many times you may not even leave; just be watchful because you could turn your head and someone, male or female, slips some dangerous object in your drink.

In today's society, some males are watching females to see whom they can devour. Such males do not want a steady mate or may already have one but just want to have a good time with another. If they feel that they may not stand a chance with you, for example, some of them may cross the line and drug your drink. Therefore, beware and be wise. Yet there is still another group of males that may be married but merely looking for some fresh meat to sample. They also attend these gatherings to see if there are some females whom they can seduce. I do not think you would want to be the other woman. Check the male out if he approaches you at a social gathering. Watch him and read between the lines. Some are very slick. They may be looking good, smelling good, and saying exactly what you want to hear. Remember, most married men have had more practice understanding women because of their close relationship with their wives. These men may seem more sensitive and considerate of your needs. Do not allow yourself to be bulldozed by their goodness because they may be using you just as a sex partner on the side. Screen, screen, and screen the guys whom you meet at these places, for some may have hidden programs that you know nothing about. I am not putting men down; I just want you to be cautious.

Going to a club to meet a guy for a possible long term marital relationship is really not the best way. Most people are there just to have a good time. A man who is sincere about a woman and their future will be honest with her. He will not mind divulging to her his medical records, income, and any other thing that she wants to know. Also, such a man does not sneak around to be with her or lie to her. And he does not mind being seen with her anytime and anywhere. Social gatherings are good, and they are necessary points of interest. Everyone, especially a woman, needs release from tension and stress, and that can be accomplished through social gatherings. And, who knows, you might just strike the right note with the right man at one of such gatherings and be hooked with him for life (in holy matrimony).

CHAPTER THREE

CHAPTER THREE
RESPECT YOURSELF

A. Self-Worth
B. Love Yourself
C. Refuse to Be Used

Chapter 3: Respect Yourself

What is the meaning of respect? Is it getting a lot of sexy looks from men? I do not think so. Respect is all about believing in yourself—knowing that you have plenty of self-worth; being able to love yourself; and, most importantly, refusing to be used.

A. Self-Worth

After we are born, our parents, in most cases, nurture us and make us feel wanted and beautiful. As we continue to grow, they show us that we are important and that we can be whatever we want to be. As I look around, I see some women who feel they are nobody and seem to have very little desire to succeed. How sad this is because it should not be so. From childhood to adulthood, something drastic happens that makes these women feel this way. It is neither the looks nor the dress alone that should make a person feel important. It is the inside that counts more.

Some women take delight in putting others down. Ladies, never let anyone lower your self-worth. When you see this happening, you better believe that the person who is constantly doing the put-downs actually admires and wants something you have. If girls get love and respect at home and are made to feel beautiful from their fathers, I do not believe they will be so apt to crave such approval from the men within their outside sphere. However, even if a girl does not receive such attention from her dad, the mother can help her to realize that she is still a gift to the world because God made her special. Young as well as older females should develop their interests and put their energies into other things that are beneficial to them.

B. Love Yourself

Basically, you must be willing to pamper, admonish, cherish, adore, and appreciate yourself. Loving yourself means you are in complete harmony with your metabolism. It does not mean you should be so pompous that you cannot stand yourself. If you cannot love yourself, how do you expect others to love you? Indeed, you must value your independence— the ability to be in control of you and to make decisions for yourself based on your feelings and concept of the matter under consideration. And do not expect others to love you as much as you love yourself because they might not see what you see. You may see charm and grace as well as intelligence and understanding in yourself, where as they might not have a clue of who you really are.

What is on the outside should never count more than what is on the inside of you. This saying is true; however, it does not mean anything if you do not believe it. If you see yourself as unloved, your self-concept will drop very low. What sustains one in life is the belief that he or she is worthy. Therefore, the more accepting you are of yourself, the more you will have a tendency to love yourself. Loving yourself, however, does not mean getting gratification from putting others down thereby building up yourself. It certainly does not mean finding the shortcomings that others possess and pointing them out. To love yourself also means to reach out and touch someone else. Spreading good will makes many people feel better about themselves in the long run.

C. Refuse to Be Used

Many times some women make the mistake of allowing others to use them. Maybe this happens as a result of looking for love and mistaking doing things for others as love. Help people when they are in need, but needlessly doing things for them is counter productive. If a female has to buy a man for him to spend time with her, then she is off base. How does she try to buy a man? Well, how about paying his rent and utilities, taking him shopping, constantly cooking his food, paying for his beeper, and just giving him money? Please a good husband (with whom you share everything) is worthy of such, not a boyfriend. I am not asking you not to reach out to your boyfriends when they are truly in need, but some women are so afraid of losing them that they are willing to go without their own basic needs in order to provide almost all they have to satisfy their boyfriends.

When you meet a guy, watch out and see if he expects money from you or asks you for money. Do you honestly want to be his sugar mama? Sometimes, he may even take your money and goods and give them to other females. A perspective marriage partner should simply enjoy being with you and you with him, even if all you two do is walk around the park or have lunch at a local restaurant. Money and other material things should not play a greater role in a relationship.

Material objects will not last, but a relationship built on mutual respect and compatibility just might. Save your body for his exploration until after marriage. If he presses you for a sample, then I say he does not respect you or love you but might only want to use you. A relationship extends beyond the physical; and, too many times, when females meet men and date them, copulation seems to be achieved too easily. This mating aspect should be the climax to the relationship—when the two truly become one! There is time to get intimate. Why are you rushing? Our society seems to hold the concept that sex is okay as long as the two partners are in "love." Well, this love seems to be short lived for many females after they engage in pre-marital sex. I am here to say that you are worth a ring on your finger and a marriage certificate.

There may be many women, of course, who are also eager to get the male in bed and may not desire to be married; however, whether they realize it or not, using is still going on. The more men with whom a woman has sex, the more other men know how easily accessible she is, so they would always want to take advantage of her; and, sooner or later, her reputation in the community would be in ruin. No decent man, I do not care what he tells you, wants to choose a sluttish woman as a life mate. Sometimes men may ask a female how many men she has had sex with. In the relationship, the woman may be tempted to answer this question. Please do not! Even if you say two, three, four, five, or ten, his idea of your value may go down. The number is not important. What is important is that you must now start loving yourself, regardless of how you may have allowed yourself to be used in the past. Wipe the slate clean and start afresh. You might not be a virgin, but you can still have pride in yourself. Even if you have children out of wedlock, do not give up on your dreams and aspirations. Some men feel that if you have a child or children, you should be willing and eager to have sex with them on request. Do not allow anyone to lower you to that level. Let the person know that you are somebody, and if he is still not ready to accept you on that level, kick him to the curb (not literally) and move on with pride. Remember, you are a princess, a queen. Accept yourself on that high level, and others will, eventually, also.

CHAPTER FOUR

CHAPER FOUR
UNDERSTANDING MEN

A. Biological Make-up

B. Desires/Aspirations

C. Men's Concept of Women: Survey

Chapter 4: Understanding Men

In order to understand men better, it is first important to understand yourself. You must decide what you want in a man and then you can understand him. There are many types of men in this world: pretty men, robust men, henpecked men, and gentlemen. When you know what type you want, then you have your pick of them.

Let's talk about the pretty men. These men are always concerned about their appearance. They believe that they are God's gift to the world. And that is okay. They spend a lot of money on themselves, buying costly cologne, designer shoes, and clothes. Depending on the amount of money they have, they may also buy expensive cars and houses. When they ask you out to dinner, they will pick the classiest restaurant to show off themselves and their dates. You will find that they are always seeking ways to improve your appearance so you can match theirs. Don't be surprised when they tell you to comb your hair a certain way and to dress a certain way so they can be proud of you in public. In a way, this can be a good thing, but after a while, you might start finding such a relationship bothersome. These men also like to keep their houses clean. Everything is in place; indeed, they may not even have dirty socks on the floor. Their dishes are clean, and their beds are always made. If your goal is to marry a pretty man, then you must decide to keep yourself immaculate and your house spotless.

The robust men, on the other hand, are all male. They like doing manly things like boxing, wrestling, and playing football. Some are even urban cowboys, and others like fixing and building things around the house. They are not as concerned with gorgeous dressing as the pretty men. Do not get me wrong; robust men will, of course, dress for an occasion or a special event. Even though they may dress in clean clothes everyday, they are more relaxed. These men like for their women to be daring and sports inclined, and they may spend more time at the gym lifting weights than at home. If you choose such a man, be prepared to wash and clean because they don't mind sweating. However, they are fun to be around. With these men, you can be yourself without putting on airs. But don't get too relaxed because they like pretty well kept women also. Robust men like cars, and they drive semi-fast, so working on their cars is another foray that these men may have, and they desire home cooked meals because they like to eat.

Another category is henpecked men. These ones never stand up for themselves. They can be bossed around and tend to like it. They dress okay but do not seem to be motivated to buy in-fashion clothes or even to cash their own checks if they work. If you choose such a man, be prepared to make most of the major decisions about household activities. However, these men can be slightly stubborn and temperamental at times.

The gentlemen group is the one that most women widely accept. They are very eclectic, which means that they adopt some traits from all the other types of men, and that makes the gentlemen group pretty amazing. They normally come on strong and maintain their stamina. They will wine and dine and pay more attention to their dates. They will open doors and compliment their dates on their appearance without focusing on flaws. These men have steady jobs and do not mind spending money on the ladies. They dress well, without being extravagant. They smell good and appreciate their female company. Their homes are well kept, without necessarily being spotless. You may find a few shoes or socks around but all in good taste. When a female is with a gentleman, she feels like a princess because he treats her as someone important. If this is the type of man you want, then follow the steps to improve yourself in terms of dress and attitude. He also appreciates a woman who is intelligent and has a decent job. When you choose this type of man, make sure that you are independent because he expects a partner, not a freeloader.

A. Biological Make-Up

Many women also get themselves into trouble because even if they understand their own bodies, they fail to understand how the male body operates. In the course of an intimate relationship, they may find themselves pregnant and unwed. So they wonder, "How did this happen?" Well, first of all, the male body is not that complicated to understand. Once you know his biological makeup, then you are able to control the situation.

Here it goes. The male body is composed of several parts, of course, but the major ones for this discussion are the penis, urethra, vas deferens, scrotum, and testes. The penis is the organ through which the release of sperms takes place. During sexual intimacy, the penis is inserted into the female vagina. He ejaculates sperms, or male sex cells, into the female passage. Sperms are released from the testes, which are stored in the scrotum. These sperms move along in the male body through the vas deferens, which are similar to the fallopian tubes in the female. Once the male injects the sperms into the female vagina, they travel, looking for an egg. If a sperm connects with a female sex cell or egg, fertilization takes place. In order to avoid this happening, make sure that you do not engage in any pre-marital sex (or as those who advocate pre-marital sex would tell you, protect yourself with some type of birth control).

B. Desires /Aspirations

Most men have desires and aspirations. These can range anywhere from being a truck driver to a medical doctor. Whatever the man aspires to be, the female's job is to find out what the man's desire is and how it relates to hers. Also, most men already have a prototype of their ideal woman in their minds, or they will select one who is compatible. If you happen to be that type of woman, then success in the marriage can easily be foretold.

A survey of university men and other males yielded ideas of the types of women guys desire to marry. There were several age groups of men surveyed, ranging from 18-47 years. I will proceed to share this information with you; and, hopefully, it will be of help when you meet the right man for marriage.

C. Men's Concept of Women: Survey Comments 1

Men's (Ages 18-47) Concept of the Ideal Woman:

WHAT IS YOUR CONCEPT OF THE IDEAL WIFE?

(Note: Each asterisk* represents a different point of view.)

*She should be ambitious and honest. Also, should be mature enough and decent. She must be respectful to my family and friends. She should also know how to communicate and manage money fairly.

*1. First, she has to have God in her heart. (Very important)
 2. She has to be sophisticated

 3. High self-esteem

 4. Likes to be involved with the community

 5. She likes to workout so she can look attractive and she can live a healthy life

6. Education-college degree

7. Outgoing, happy, likes to vote

*Strong emotionally with confidence and intelligence

*A woman who is smart, determined, pretty, funny, from 18-25 years old. Someone who always wants to have a good time. Respects me as well as herself. Has a good personality. I would also want her to be faithful.

*Pretty (legs, feet, hair, and nails) and of course smart, honest, willing to do whatever I ask of her. Has goals for the future, who has not been with a lot of men, one who is close to her family

*5 feet 10 inches tall
135-145 pounds
Long, silky black hair
Bright skinned
Big breasts
Tight buns

*A woman with an education and a degree, someone smart, good-looking and down right fine

*I would like to marry someone who is smart and knows how to have fun. Must be considerate of my needs.

*Independent, intelligent woman who is secure and has lots of confidence in herself

*Highly sophisticated, with academic or professional power, a good dresser. Any race will do for me. Not so thin neither too fat; about 5 feet 10 inches in height.

*I would like to marry a woman who is reasonable but is not too conservative and on the other hand not too liberal. She should also be somebody who respects me and loves me as a person and not because of what I have.

*A nice lady about my height and it really doesn't matter what her skin color is if she is dark skinned or yellow skinned. She has to have an education, graduated from high school at least and maybe in college. I think a well- educated woman will work out very well. I will not marry out of my skin color. She has to have major goals in life.

*My ideal woman would have to be a very attractive black woman. She would be an intellectual; she should be able to cook and clean. She would have to be easy to get along with and be able to satisfy me sexually.

*The ideal woman would be a pretty nice looking young lady inside and out. Not afraid to speak her true feelings, even when in doubt. Would

stand up for her man even when he is wrong. Intelligence would be an important factor in my choosing the ideal woman!

*I would love to have a woman between the age of 23-26 who makes a whole lot of money$$(Blonde)

*She would be very special. She would be very smart, caring, also nice looking. She would have to have a great personality.

*A woman well brought up
Good manners
A woman with a college degree

*Funny, outgoing, intelligent, very agreeable, beautiful eyes, wonderful smile, loves me for who I am, and can put up with my attitude or me.

*A woman who dresses nicely and does not use foul language. She has to have good morals and values.

*A woman who knows what she wants and expresses how she really feels. She also needs to tell me when I do something that she does not like. She needs to put me in my place when I act up, yet be kind. She needs to be nice but does not let me run over her.

*The woman I like to marry is a woman that is nice, looks good (model) about 6 feet 3 inches. She should have long hair and packing in all the right places. Last of all not bossy and never cheats

*I don't want a wife. I just want a sex buddy.

*Nice, honest and likes doing things, going out and having fun. Someone I love and respect and who can do some things for me.

*An independent, strong woman—intelligent and loving.

*The ideal woman for me would be one who respects herself and be-lieves in God. Also, she must respect and accept me for me. She must

also have a great personality and be very spontaneous. She must be a well-rounded woman who wants to achieve.

*My ideal woman would be, first of all, wealthy, pretty, smart, and sweet

*My ideal woman must have beautiful eyes and a good personality. She cannot be a girl that complains or gripes too much.

*Just like me
5 feet, 5 inches, blonde or brown hair,
Thin body, big breasts, and big butt

*My ideal woman would be tall, redheaded, green-eyed, and beautiful. She would be caring, nice, understanding, and very passionate. She should also have a great personality and be very considerate.

*The ideal wife would be loving, intelligent, and beautiful. A woman who carries herself with dignity. Someone who is giving, not selfish. A woman who can carry on every kind of conversation. She would be funny or serious.

*The ideal woman for me would have a terrific sense of humor. She would be very loving, caring, and compassionate. She would be a woman of high intelligence and must be independent; she should also be able to stand-alone.

*Sensitive and caring, and knows what she wants out of life, but not afraid to have some fun. She should have knowledge of the value of a dollar. Many women today do not value a dollar. Hopefully, she is energetic and likes to be a little daring at times. Open to new ideas and willing to con-sider other people's ideas and feelings as well.

*Smart, good personality, common sense, pretty, kind, and likes herself.

*I believe the ideal woman for me should be:
1. A churchgoer
2. Be able to put up with a coach

3. Realistic

4. Willing to let me hang out with friends

*I think the ideal woman will be 0-3 years older or younger than I am. She will be very spontaneous and enjoy doing off-the-wall things. She must be a good cook and considerate with money. Divorce will not be an option in our marriage. She will dress nicely but a little conservative. She must be willing to be very family oriented.

*One who especially loves God above all other things.
One who is attractive in looks, yet very caring to others and me
One who enjoys being with my family and is able to compromise. She must not be conceited. She must like to do things outside. Be clean (housekeeper), cooks well, and must be considerate with money (she must budget).

*A woman who can cook, keep house clean, and keep herself looking decent. I want a woman that understands that I like to hunt and fish, but I don't like to shop. Must also have a sense of humor, and living in the country with lots of hunting dogs. Must also have childbearing hips.

*I would like my wife to be understanding, outgoing, funny, and sexy in her own way. I would not want her trying to conform to the modern society all of the time. I just want her to be herself.

*Cook
Clean house
Look pretty

*The ideal wife is a woman who is not afraid to speak her mind. She can be serious but also funny. She would also need to be athletic but not to the point of being manish.

*I would like my wife to be very distinguished and respectful. She should be well educated and maintain a suitable job. I would like her to be nice. I would also like her to handle herself in all situations that she may encounter.

*One that is proud of herself and myself. One that respects my ideas and doesn't complain too much or tell me what to do. Someone who is an eye catcher. Smart and can carry a conversation with someone.

*I believe the ideal woman is a person who respects herself. She is a Christian lady who loves her husband and kids. She gives in, yet she stands her ground. She does not need to be a slob.

*A woman of the same faith as me, who will help me to remain faithful. A woman of good maturity; one who does not curse or use drugs and is not rude. She must have some of the same interests, but not all of my interests. She must desire to stay in shape and maintain a healthy lifestyle. She must also be a hard worker.

*I have a wife; she is perfect enough.

*5 feet 10 inches and to die for! Long hair, nice skin, big butt, and brains.
*My concept of a real and ideal woman/lady is one who has intelligence and uses it. Beauty is limited to my concept of the perfect lady; attitude and the need and drive to succeed go a long way when I choose a loving lady. She must share the following qualities with me:
a. Modesty
b. Honesty
c. Cognitive ability

*She should be a Christian, humble, beautiful, understanding, helpful, encouraging, forgiving, loving, and intelligent and all the positive things that have not been mentioned.

*My concept of the ideal woman would be: one that is nice looking and just doesn't gripe so much. Women just seem to nag the hell out of me.

*A woman who knows God personally. A Christian woman.

*Ladylike in all ways

Have high morals
Good personality
Likes to do fun things
Sweet, kind, and loving

*Christian
Athletic build
Nice smile
Good sense of humor
Intelligent
Affectionate

*Quiet
Level headed
Loving
Likes the same things as I do
On time

*The ideal woman for a wife is a person that is very responsible, mature, and hard working. A person that can give love and take love is very important. A woman must be able to organize and deal with a husband in a tactful way. Never Nag. Always be able to communicate with her spouse and never feels sorry for herself. The perfect wife is a woman who is not selfish and cares about God and an eternal life!

*The ideal woman would be someone who will take care of her husband and kids (if any). The husband should love her and be kind to her.

*Physical attractiveness is important, but most important to me is a woman's loyalty. She must be willing to compromise some. She needs to be happy with herself.

   As you can see, there are common attributes that most men are looking for when they proceed to get married. Many women, I believe, already have most of the traits that these men are looking for. This information gives an inside view of what men consider marriage material. In order to get married, try exhibiting more of these traits because men know what they want; and, in most cases, they are the ones doing the asking.

C. Survey Comments 2

Another survey of men ages 18-47 yielded some interesting facts. One may wonder what men think of women. Well, the following are questions and men's responses that I want to share with you:

Question #1: Do you believe that most women like or value themselves?
Answer: 69 percent believed that most women do like and value themselves
                      26 percent believed most women do not
                      5 percent were undecided

Question #2 Do you believe most women seem to have specific goals for themselves?
Answer: 84 percent believed
                      15 percent did not believe
                      1 percent was undecided

Question #3 How are women dressing today: classical, sleazy, or sloppy?
Answer: 40 percent believed women are dressing classical
                      37 percent believed women are dressing sleazy
                      19 percent said women are dressing sloppy
                      4 percent were undecided

Question #4 Should a female's skirt be knee length, thigh length, or panty line length?
Answer: 42 percent preferred a female's skirt should be knee length
                      52 percent said it should be thigh length
                      6 percent said it should be panty line length

Question #5 Do you think women are unladylike if they use curse words?
Answer: 61 percent thought it is unladylike for a woman to use curse words
                      39 percent thought it is not unladylike for a woman to use curse words

Though only five questions were asked to get a feel for men's perception of women, I believe some of the issues are valid. The only way for a female to know what a man appreciates is for her to sit and have a conversation with him. Communication is the key to understanding what a man desires and what he appreciates. I hope this information can be of benefit to you when you meet the right man with whom to share your life.

PART II

PLAIN TALK FOR WOMEN: TIPS FOR STAYING MARRIED

CHAPTERS FIVE AND SIX

CHAPTER FIVE

A. Being Married
B. Happiness
C. Love
D. Money
E. Togetherness

Chapter 5:
A. Being married

Marriage symbolizes wholeness. It means that you are into the relationship, and your desires or aspirations become intertwined with another person's. In this situation, the couple must substitute I for we. The single entity of oneness has evaporated. Being married is a joyous state for one to be in; it is a relationship consummated with God's blessings. Therefore, one cannot think of himself or herself as footloose and fancy free. The two persons involved in the marriage must consort with each other daily to maintain their harmonious relationship. Being married, in simplistic terms, is like two people being on a Ferris wheel, clasping each other's hand as tightly as they can with the intention of never letting go. Some may also compare marriage to bungee jumping. You have the high, and you jump but with the assurance that you will eventually land safely, as long as you have your protective attachment.

In the marriage situation, you have your partner or life mate. Regardless of the ups and downs, hold on to each other, and you both will land safely. In this instance, the bungee rope is God, who will anchor you safely in the marriage. Being married means that you are in constant subjugation to the other partner. It is an intertwining of mind, heart, body, and soul. All too often partners try to identify with one of the elements aforementioned instead of combining all into their relationship. All elements must be mixed in order to be truly married. It is similar to baking a cake. If all the necessary ingredients are not included and mixed well, the cake will not turn out right.

Being married is caring equally about the other person as you care about yourself; marriage consists of two individuals, male and female, who have legally committed themselves to each other. This is about as close as you can get to the next person. If the two parties join their spirits, then marriage can become a permanent state of being. It is one of the keys to joyous living. Sharing the essence of marriage is a worthwhile experience destined to bring happiness, eliminating a battle of wills and making for a cohesive existence. Indeed, marriage is a state in which one person relinquishes his or her control over the other in a meaningful way. True marriage should also encompass such issues as happiness, love, money, and togetherness.

B. Happiness

In order for couples to be happy, they must first understand what happiness is all about; then they can strive to be in harmony with each other. What makes one happy, indeed? The meaning of true happiness seems to elude many people from all races and status. Can happiness be based on inanimate objects, such as cars, houses, and degrees? Well, some people may say so, and some may go even further to make the world believe so. Could happiness be a facade? Let us look at the whole situation.

You were extremely happy when you were young, give or take some of us. Happiness came from watching mommy and daddy say kind words to each other. This made you feel secure and safe. Giving things to relatives whom you cared about made you happy. However, much of that happiness changed as you got older. Now, it seems as if it takes more out of you to make you happy. People like to shop for many hours, and they think this makes them happy. Nevertheless, after shopping, on leaving the store, they think about other things they should have bought or needed to buy, and a chunk of their previous happiness diminishes.

I have come to the conclusion that one cannot buy happiness. Happiness is a state of mind. If you ever regain the happiness that you had during your youth, hang on to it for your dear life. Now, as a couple, I believe you want to know how to get happiness. The truth is very simple: accept Christ whole-heartedly into your lives, and He will make you glad. He will give you a calm, peaceful heart and will have you looking toward the present and future with glee instead of concentrating upon past mistakes and failures.

C. Love

In any marriage, love is the key. It is also the glue that holds couples together. Love is the magic that sparkles throughout the relationship. Without it, the kaleidoscope is dull and eventually creates disinterest for the couple. Knowing that love holds the marriage together is not enough. We need a working definition for love. I believe love is an internal feeling that starts at the bottom of your toes and extends to your scalp. If you are looking for this, then you are sadly mistaken. Love is a genuine desire to see the other person in the relationship truly happy. It is a deep-seated understanding that everything will not be perfect in the relationship. Proverbs 10:12 says that love covers every sin.

Therefore, love means forgiving your partner even if he or she has done something wrong in the marriage. It is admitting that the person is special even at his or her worst exhibition of negative behavior. Love is all about cherishment. In other words, you are going to treat that person fragilely, just as you handle glass with care. Love is believing in the individual, even though life has thrown him or her some debilitating curves. It is not bailing out at the first sign of trouble; it is not walking away because the road got a little rocky. Love is kind, caring, and understanding. It is the dream maker for another's endeavors. Love is not ridicule—tearing the partner to shreds because of slip-ups or demeaning acts.

Love goes with marriage as peanut butter goes with jelly. Love is not cold hearted or domineering; it is not discord or estrangement. Neither is it singleness of mind. Love is a uniting of joy at being bound to another person. It creates a glow that grows brighter with each passing day. Love is the pollen that bees cannot exist without; it is the opposite of hate and confusion. It is the cinnamon and nutmeg that go in a sweet potato pie, leaving a lasting aroma in the kitchen long after the pie is cooked. Love can withstand negative criticism from the other party.

In fact, love is a word that is often used too lightly. It is not a passing fancy to disarm other human beings so they allow their guards to slip. It should not be used as a transmitter to prove a point. Love is a bright beam that extends from the heart. It also has a tendency to purify a heart that is black by making it white as snow. In a marriage, when partners love each other truly, no mountain is too high, no sickness is too morbid, and no deed is too unforgivable. Love is not a blockage that refuses passage from one polarity to the other; it is a commitment to stay together until the end. Look within yourself and examine the extent of your love for your partner. If it does not cover much ground, then you must strive to expound your love for the person you took in holy matrimony, incorporating aspects that will extend the life of your marriage because love that comes from the soul is the most important ingredient in a marriage. . Without love, the marriage will crumble like a piece of toast or melt like a snowflake at the least sign of heat.

Enclosed is a little poem that my husband wrote for me during our first few years of marriage. I thought I should share it with you.

Unbreakable Bond

By Japhet N. Makia

My love for you never shall perish,
for you are my treasure of endless
joy and the nectar of my life.
A stream of love through our veins
flows and will forever keep us fresh.
Two lovers, by God so knotted,
can neither man nor Devil break apart.
And if one by Death is taken, the other must in faith
live, for the partner's love will forever dwell within.

As you can see, this poem practically summarizes the points I was
making about love.

D. Money

Too many couples get entangled with disputes over money. What's the fuss? Money should not occupy such a huge chunk in the marriage because it is just a means to an end. We use money to pay bills and buy material things, nothing more. It should not be used as a power tool. Well, what do I mean by that? I am saying that if one partner works and makes more money than the other, he/she should not see that as a controlling factor. Some men have ego problems concerning money, and that attitude stems from society's stigma that the male should be the major breadwinner; otherwise, he is not a man. Some partners believe that if one makes more money than the other, his/her point of view concerning money matters is supreme. Get a grip; a marriage is not based on dollars but total commitment. Money matters should be shared equally among the partners.

Couples, if both of you work, count that as a blessing. Pool your resources and share in the household management. If you come together over money issues, try to identify financial problems that your home may be facing. In today's marriages, most couples have two separate bank accounts where they make financial transactions separately. This is okay if that is the way both of you want it. However, sometimes when couples have a joint account where they discuss money transactions together, there may be more harmony within the relationship. When this joint monetary procedure is done, there is a feeling of togetherness and unity. (I am speaking from experience.) Partners should consort with each other before they make major purchases because this shows a sign of mutual respect for each other.

In some relationships, however, one spouse may choose not to work for money but may decide to stay home as a homemaker. This situation is not so strange. Nevertheless, discussions between partners about financial matters should still be a two-party decision-making process.

Both spouses should give serious consideration to wise financial management so money does not become a block in their marriage. Couples should also weigh their credits as well as financial investments. Basically, manage your money wisely together.

E. Togetherness

Remember when you were dating? It was exciting to walk hand in hand with your partner. Your heart was probably racing excitedly when you would go to the movies, skating rink, or even just to a social gathering. Being together was the major requirement for happiness. You felt sad and out of sync when the other party did not call or come over to visit. The feeling of being together was warm and comforting. Even though you had arguments, making up was easy because you missed the camaraderie of being together. In marriage, togetherness should be even stronger than when you were dating because your feelings for each other should be much more than before.

As a married couple, you have more times to be in disagreement, but making up should come more easily than before because you have had a lot of time to study the behavior patterns of your partner. Spending time together in a marriage is super important. Sometimes couples get so caught up in their everyday lives that they forget the most significant ingredient that will make the marriage work, togetherness. Set aside time to be together. Work outside the home can be very demanding, but house (or at home) chores can be equally demanding. If there are kids involved, then you need even more time in order for you to take care of their demands.

Nevertheless, you were a couple before most of these outside demands were placed upon your time together. Relax, life will keep going if you set aside some time each day to find out how each other is doing. Being together helps a couple remember the love, joy, and respect that you have for one another. Bring the sparkle into your life that was there when you were dating. Go to places together. A lack of being together will cause couples to grow apart, gradually, from each other. The more you are together, the deeper the love for each other will flow. Don't make the mistake of spending more time with other people than with each other. Go for lovely walks together. Peace and tranquility in the relationship will come to the forefront. Call each other up at work sometimes just to say, "Hello, darling." Send each other flowers. Heh, once in a while, take each other out for a quiet lunch or dinner. Little gestures like these will help glue couples together. Kind words for each other and understanding will also help a marriage stay together.

CHAPTER SIX

CHAPTER SIX

A. Spirituality
B. Sexual Fulfillment
C. Family
D. Friends
E. Work
F. Entertainment

Marriage Survey

1. Female Views
2. Male Views

A. Spirituality

The essence of spirituality is to have a deep-seated belief in God. Many people get married without adequately addressing the issue of Christianity. They are not aware of the power of Christ in their lives. Then in times of crisis, they have no source of strength because of their lack of a foundation in God. In fact, some couples don't know how to handle Christianity in the home, especially if both belong to different religions. This can lead to a sense of discord. Yet other couples handle such a situation beautifully.

Going to church regularly can give couples a sense of peace and strength within the home. Some people may say they have peace without going to church. Maybe so; nevertheless, church can be a place of calming enjoyment. It gives the couple a chance to mingle with other Christians and experience true love that stems from a common belief in the Almighty God. Christianity should not be a source for disunity at home. One partner may think that his/her religion is better than the other. This can quickly lead to disagreement and disunity. Even though a difference in religious beliefs should have been ironed out before the marriage, if such a situation occurs, sit down and discuss the matter rationally. Probably the couple should visit each other's church periodically and study the Bible constantly together at home. Spirituality is more than just going to church, though; it is a supreme desire to love each other honestly with God's blessings. Serenity is at the forefront of Christianity. One must constantly keep one's thoughts and actions geared toward an acceptance by the Supreme Being.

A holy matrimony also means that you, the couple, must have a home base from which you can draw inner strength as you face the tidal waves of loneliness, grief, and marital problems. Your partner is not going to do everything right all the time, but the Holy Spirit in you will give you the resilience to overcome his/her antics and help the relationship resume smooth sailings (as long as your partner, too, is willing to submit herself/himself to God's power). Spirituality also means that you are able to accept each other's strengths and weaknesses. Build on your partner's strengths, and work hard to mitigate problems that might arise from the weaknesses. If you do this, you will be in sync with your spouse and with the world around you.

B. Sexual Fulfillment

Intimacy, of course, is a significant part of any marriage. Each partner should show love toward the other. This can be done in the form of making love or copulation. No one can tell a married couple how often to make love; that would be unrealistic. Nevertheless, sexual relationship brings the two together so that they function as one. Early in the marriage, because of the newness of the relationship, couples may find themselves seeking sexual gratification from each other more often. They may tend to make love two, three, four, or five times a week. Some may go as far as expressing love in public, maybe in the form of kissing, petting, or hugging. They may gaze longingly into each other's eyes, sending a silent message that later, romance will take place. Romance helps keep the relationship solid. A touch, a look, or a smile does wonders in a marriage, indicating that the partners are still attractive to each other.

As the years go by in several marriages, however, the intimate looks, petting, hugging, and kissing may dwindle. This tears down the marriage. People in this less romantic state tend to pull away from each other. When this happens, sex comes to a halt. Who wants to make love to someone who never seems to appreciate him or her? Sexual fulfillment is more than the act of performing sex; it is the totality of deep feelings for each other. Never lose the drive or desire to explore sexually with your partner. Communicate to him or her what really turns you on.

Okay, so one partner may be more timid than the other; take that into consideration. Be understanding. Talk about the problem and try to resolve your differences so that sex flows smoothly. If one partner has problems relating to the other about sex, seek the advice of a counselor or sex therapist, and work hard to resolve your differences. Sometimes medical attention is needed to correct a sexual based problem. Consult your family doctor, read books, watch movies. Do whatever it takes to make that part of your relationship as comfortable and easy as holding hands, walking, and breathing. An exceptional case may be found among couples who are in their golden years—couples whose sexual desire for each other may have been curtailed by nature. That is not bad because God, in His wisdom, made it so. Maybe it is His way of telling such senior citizens that it is now time for them to concentrate all of their faculties heavenward as they draw closer to be with Him in His kingdom.

C. Family

Most couples are apprehensive about each other's relatives. Regardless of how many he/she has, they should be considered a part of the family. Therefore, we have a duty to get along with them as best we can. Many relatives support marriage, so they often offer good advice to the married couple, encouraging and providing help, especially to the young couple.

Nevertheless, some families can also be detrimental to the marriage. This happens when a spouse forgets where his/her loyalty lies. Pleasing your mom, dad, brothers, and sisters is not bad, but the major person you must please the most is your spouse. The two of you can still have a good working relationship with family members on both sides. However, if you have a close relationship with your parents and siblings, your spouse should not feel threatened. There is enough room in a human heart to have love for your spouse as well as for your family. If family members have a tendency to dictate into the marriage, then that spouse should sit and converse with the members and ask them to stop the dictation.

Families should reach out to the newly married couple, acting as anchors, especially during trying times. There should be a sense of unity and togetherness on both sides of the family; no one family should believe they are better than the other. And for you parents, do not become Shakespeare's King Lear who wanted his three daughters to make a public declaration of their total love for him; when his youngest daughter, Cordelia—who was more honest than the other two daughters—said she would love him as any child would love a father but that she would keep a part of her love for the husband she would marry, Old Lear, in his ignorance, cast away the only daughter who truly loved him. So, spouses, communicate with your families and let them know that even though you still and will always love and care for them, your spouse comes first. You intend to love him/her "till death do you part."

D. Friends

Before one gets married, he/she has a circle of friends who, normally, are lifelong. Some may wonder if it is necessary to sever all ties with friends of the opposite sex. Well, what do you think? Do you want your male or female friend with whom you might have had sexual relations or for whom you had feelings calling your marital home? I don't believe such a situation would be very healthy. Or why would you want to maintain close friendships with someone to whom you were physically attracted before you got married? I am not saying that because you are married, you should not have friends. What I am stressing on is that you and your spouse should have friends who are neutral to any past conquests or hopes of conquests. We need friends in a marriage. However, never make the mistake of using your friends to ridicule your partner. That is not the duty of a friend. True friends sometimes give encouragement to couples who are facing difficult situations, and friends can form a recreational group to help the couple relieve the stresses of everyday living.

E. Work

Work is important in everyone's life because it is a means to an end. It is something one must do in order to survive. When people get married, they still have work obligations. One must not forget, however, that work is not the only primery thing that determines one's existence. Therefore, a partner should not use work as an excuse to stay away from home for long periods of time. It should also not be used as a leverage maker. Sometimes couples get so involved with their jobs that they tend to forget the most important aspect of the marriage—being together. Couples should also not use work as a place for complete relaxation. It doesn't help your marriage if you are completely relaxed at work but tensed at home. Indeed, it is at home where you should relax and unwind.

Also, your coworkers should not take the place of your spouse. You get up in the morning and dress up well mainly to look attractive to your coworker. How would your spouse feel when he/she realizes that your main purpose for dressing so well is to impress an "important" person at your job? Do you really need that type of attention? It is your spouse whom you should impress because that is the person to whom you said, "I Do." Be cordial to your coworkers, however, but never forget that is all they are—coworkers. Should a married person flirt with co-workers? Some people may say it is okay as long as one keeps the flirtation innocent. Explain to me how you are going to keep flirting mean-ingless. I say save that for your spouse so both of you may remain de-voted to each other. Again, work is a good place where you contribute your talents to society and earn a living, not an environment in which you drag your home life down the drain. In other words, work is not a place where you discuss your family problems, because you do not want to be the topic of discussion in the break room. How do you think your spouse would feel at the job's Christmas party, for example, realizing that every-one there knows exactly how many disagreements the two of you have had at home and what they were about?

A marriage between two people should be kept that way and not become part of a cooperative hotline. If a problem arises in your mar-riage, try to resolve it yourselves harmoniously. If it is too complex, ask for help from close family members (including preachers, elders and dea-cons). You can also seek the advice of marriage counselors. Couples should, however, share their happy or sad experiences at their jobs with each other. Go home at the end of the day and discuss with each other how your day went. Sit down and have some conversation about each other's workday before you move on to more important matters. When the job starts to demand more than its fair share in your lives, reevaluate the work situation and come up with ways to reduce the amount of time one or both of you spend at work. As partners, you should not become jealous of each other's work, though, but communicate constantly with your partner about your job, encouraging each other as needed.

F. Entertainment

Couples should not spend all of their time working; they should incorporate recreation into their busy schedules also. A marriage can become dull quickly if there is no room for enjoyment. The wife and husband can plan fun activities that will enhance the relationship. Events such as going to the movies, skating, or bowling cost money. But walking in the park, spending a quiet time at home watching a video, or just having a peaceful ride together are very inexpensive ways that can contribute to the couple's well being. Dating each other periodically should be an important part of a married couple's life. You can also invite friends over to share snacks with you as a form of fun, pastime activities. Taking a trip to visit relatives can also be a warm recreational activity that promotes closeness. Whatever you decide to do, do something to keep the spark of adventure.

MARRIAGE SURVEY

I conducted a survey in which I asked married couples (both husbands and wives) ranging from 5 to 62 years of marriage to separately give some tips why their marriage has lasted that long and how other couples can benefit from their wisdom. The results of the survey are as follows:

(Each asterisk represents a different point of view.)

1. Female Views

*Don't put your mate down or say hateful things. They will come back to haunt you. Stop looking around for some one else.

*Enjoy the little things—have fun with one another. Laugh together. Don't be afraid to show playful affection. Share activities, plan meals together, set up dates. Don't take each other for granted; common courtesy and mutual respect should continue no matter how long you're in a relationship. Expect change, from finances to life styles; try to resolve conflict; be open to whatever life may bring. Remember to show compassion and forgiveness. Don't expect a romantic fantasy all the time. Be understanding of what your spouse may be going through. Share common interests and goals. Keep communicating of each other's dreams and goals. Be strong in the faith. Don't try to change your spouse. Enjoy and respect each other's individuality. Share moral and ethical values. Talk about these issues both before and during a marriage and deal with difficulties together. Compromise. Each person may have a different style of coping, but be supportive of one another's opinions. Be best friends. Create a sense of togetherness like having children — building a family. Live within your means. Learn to build, not blast the self-esteem of your partner. Determine that your marriage is a gift from God and set apart by Him and designed for your happiness to last as long as you and your spouse shall live. Express your love to your mate every day.

*Don't let divorce be an option when you are not getting along. Talk about your problems. Work them out. Compromise. Both parties should be totally committed to the marriage even before the vows are made.

*1. First pray that God will send a Christian mate your way.

2. Take time to get to know what kind of person he is.

3. Long engagement — at least one year.

4. There is a cliché —The family that prays together, stays together.

5. Get marriage counseling lessons before and during the marriage- (if needed) from a Christian counselor.

6. Always start the day by saying, "I love you," and say a prayer with your mate.

7. Ask God to handle all your problems that day and leave them in His hands.

8. Never go to bed angry at one another. End the day by saying, "I love you" and praying at the end of the day.

*When my husband and I were ready for marriage, we went to a Justice of the Peace and got married. After the ceremony was over, the judge said, "Instead of you paying me a fee, I'm going to give you a gift." He opened up his desk drawer and gave us a King James Bible, and he told us, "When you are going through tough times, always use this Bible."

* 1. Learn to bend (compromise). Think about what is best for every-one, not just yourself.

2. Do not run home to Mama every time you have a spat. I've seen a lot of young marriages destroyed by this act. Stay until things are settled between you and your spouse. Just remember, your family will probably say, "I told you so." No one wants to hear that.

3. Do not tell intimate, private things about your love life to others.

This is to be kept between the two of you and is no one else's business.

4. Do not criticize your spouse in front of your family. This is hurtful and destroys a lot of respect and trust.

5. Do not flirt with anyone other than your spouse. It destroys selfesteem.

6. Do not nag.

7. Love and trust are not the same. When you love, you can't help it. But trust is earned. Try to earn your spouse's trust.

8. Compliment each other even when you are old and ugly. Even then, there is always something to compliment.

9. Be proud of your spouse and let them know how proud you are to be married to them.

10. Be affectionate and loving and show compassion when the other one is down.

11. Put God first and the rest will fall together.

12. Treat your mate as you would like to be treated.

13. If you disagree with your spouse, use tact to explain your reason. Do not make him or her feel he or she is stupid or wrong. There are usually two sides. Be willing to compromise.

14. Keep the Lord in your hearts.

*1. Keep your finances under control. Besides paying for your house and car on time, be paying with credit on only one more item at the most. Worry over money can soon erode a relationship.

2. Do not try to remake your mate. Accept, for the most part, the whole package. You married him/her for whom he/she is; don't try to make

him/her just like you.

3. Give the other partner space. It is wonderful to do things together, but sometimes each needs to do his/her own thing. Don't hold the other on too short a rope.

4. Say, "I'm sorry." Don't be so stubborn that you can't apologize or meet the other halfway.

5. Look for the good things in each other.

6. And, of course, have a Bible-based, Christian marriage, Put God/ Christ first, spouse next, and then self.

* Put Christ first (be faithful Christians)
Communication (talk things out)
Unconditional love for each other

 * Communication is the key! Without communication, you have nothing.

 * As simple as it sounds, using the Golden Rule (Do unto others as you would have them do unto you) works wonderfully in a marriage. Always treat your husband well, speak to your husband, speak about your husband as you would like for him to treat you, speak to you, speak about you. It really works. Of course, there will still be occasional hurt feelings and misunderstandings. Never let these hurt feelings linger at bedtime — never go to bed (sleep) angry with your husband. As the Bible says, "Don't let the sun go down on your wrath." It might be that you will have to agree to disagree on a certain subject, but don't let that stand in your way of saying, "I love you" every night. Enter your marriage with a <u>commitment to the marriage</u>, not the person. People change through time, and it is too easy to say, "He's not the same man I married" and use that as an excuse to divorce. Always remember that "love" is an action verb, not a state of being. "Love" is something that you do, not the way you feel. Also remember that your commitment to the marriage takes precedence over your children. (I'm not talking about an abusive relationship.) Too many young women put their children first ahead of their husbands. The

only one who should take precedence over your husband is God. The greatest gift and security you can give your children is to love their father.
* Always be understanding and considerate. If both partners put the other one's wishes first and be unselfish, the marriage will work great

* Talk to each other; resolve your differences.
Don't try to change each other.
Don't expect too much and be prepared to compromise.
Have a good relationship with your in-laws.

2. Male Views

* Be honest about your expectations even if that may hinder you from getting what you want.
Falling in love with a person's heart and soul will last much longer than their appearance.

*1. Remember your marriage vows. You were serious at the time. You really meant that you would love, cherish, and respect each other in all kinds of circumstances. If both partners agree to keep the vow you made, you will make whatever adjustments are necessary to maintain the love you felt for each other that day.

2. Respect each other's ideas, opinions, and feelings. Never criticize each other in a negative way. At times, constructive criticism may be acceptable, but it must be done with love that is so clear and obvious that it will not hurt. For example, be willing to let each other know if something displeases you. You are eager to do what pleases the person you love, and you are willing not to do what does not please the person you truly love.

3. Express love and affection freely. True love is more than emotion or feeling, it is commitment. The kind of love that is commanded in the Bible requires an act of the will, not merely emotion. That is the kind of love you vowed, before God and the witnesses present, in the marriage ceremony. You said, I WILL to these things, no matter what happens in the future!

4. Be willing to forgive and to ask for forgiveness. Do not stubbornly insist on having your way about things. If both partners are willing to adopt this attitude, things can always be worked out. Be willing to "go the extra mile."

5. Be patient with each other. Agree on what you expect of each other in every area of life.

6. Work together on a plan for handling your finances. It is a partnership, and both partners must respect the priorities agreed upon.

7. Never go to sleep at night unhappy or with anger, resentment, or any negative feelings. Have an agreement with your spouse; never go to sleep until all negative feelings are cleared. Never go to sleep without saying, "I Love You!"

8. Develop a sense of humor. Learn to laugh together.

9. Learn to communicate; talk things over. The key to good communication is seeing things from the other person's point of view, unconditional regard and acceptance, and absolute sincerity.

*1. We will find that God's laws are better for us and will help us. (Matt. 19:1-9)

2. Make commitment and strive to keep it.

3. Be able and willing to help and forgive at all times.

4. Go that second mile at all times.

5. Determine to make the marriage work and it will work.

6. Remember that your spouse is your other half and you two are now one in all things.

7. Have feeling, respect, and love for each other.

* Marriage is a give-and-take agreement
A long marriage does not just happen: it has to be worked at.
Marriage is not easy
Be willing to listen to your mate
The husband is in charge, but he doesn't have to dominate.
Only one carries the checkbook.

* Learn patience.
Bite your tongue when angry.
Put yourself in your mate's shoes.

Remember there are very few things worth fighting about.
Praise your mate often in his/her presence.

* Honor the commitment made to each other. Sometimes you may not
<u>feel</u> like staying together, but honor your commitment to each other and
make divorce non-optional.

* Develop Spirituality
Kindness and expressions of love (tenderness)
Good communication skills
Longsuffering to weaknesses
Free from pride and arrogance
Don't always place yourself ahead of your spouse
Hold hands when discussing a disagreement
Avoid jealous behavior (trust)
Be the right person and expect your love to grow
Most important, be committed to your marriage

*1. Learn the art of talking to one another.
Nothing is more critical!
Express your <u>true</u> feelings openly

2. Learn how to give of yourself.
We're far too selfish. Try to be "self-less"
You must like yourself, but try to practice
What is the essence of I Cor. 13

3. Don't keep score. Nobody will win. Try to love
unconditionally. It's not easy, but it can be mastered.

4. Commit yourself to the premise that "Marriage is Forever"
Don't consider <u>any</u> other options. (There is only one scripture reason for
divorce, adultery, none other.)

5. Remember the "little things." During the courtship period, we remember to "call," buy flowers, open the door, etc. That somehow ceases
when marriage occurs. We still like to be appreciated.

* When one of you is down, the other one needs to pick up the fallen mate. If one of you is angry, keep your cool and don't add to the matter.

Final Thoughts

It was a joy for me to write this book because life is precious. When you are given a chance for happiness with the right person, treasure him or her always. Use this book as a reference tool to answer questions that you may have concerning some issues related to getting married and staying married. May God bless each of you, and thank you for allowing me to touch a small part of your life.

Plain Talk for Women: The Key to Getting Married and Tips for Staying Married

By

Elner J. Makia

Educational Enhancement Group
Magnolia, Arkansas